THE INSTRUCTOR'S POCKETBOOK

By John Townsend

"The most creatively practical book on the subject. Even the most experienced trainer will find a handful of ideas" – Judy Simpson, Group Program Director, Management Centre Europe, Brussels.

"The Instructor's Pocketbook is an extremely useful collection of helpful hints, suggestions and reminders for instructors and presenters. It is standard handout material to all instructors we train" – Arne Luehrs, Sales Training Manager, and Richard Franklin, Dealer Training Manager, Hewlett-Packard, France.

CONTENTS

Page

INTRODUCTION

THE SUPERSTAR TEACHER/TRAINER

Personal Characteristics

- Physically fit
- Positive and optimistic attitude to life
- Pleasant voice
- Wide life experience and reading
- Open to learn from students
- Practises principles taught in class
- Eats and drinks in moderation
- Enjoys leading groups
- Socializes easily with students
- Keeps cool, manages stress effectively
- Punctual — keeps time promises and rules
- Creates and meets high expectations

Consulting Skills

- Accurate Empathy
  (shows respect and concern for students' attitudes and beliefs)

- Non-Possessive Warmth
  (Ability to create rapport with all students without favouritism or subjectivity)

- Authenticity
  (feels and appears open and relaxed, reacts genuinely and without defensiveness)

--- PRESENTATION SKILLS ---

- Possesses and practises all platform and presentation skills outlined in this pocket book

BEWARE OF THE EXPERT !

EX

SPURT

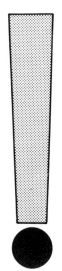

"A HAS−BEEN"

"A DRIP UNDER PRESSURE"

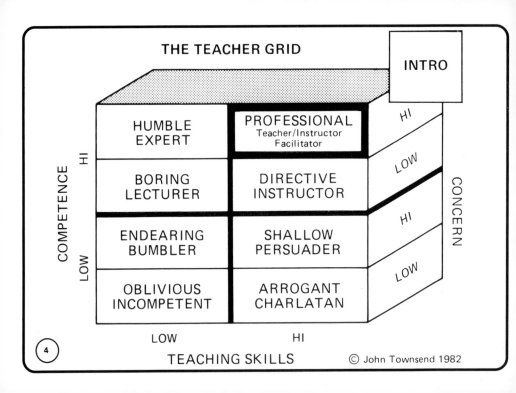

LEARNING THEORY

LEARNING THEORY

BRAINS

HOW ADULTS LEARN

- If they want and need to

- By linking learning to past, present or future experience

- By practising what they have been taught

- With help and guidance

- In an informal and non-threatening environment

BRAINS

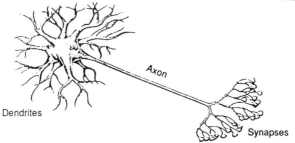

Neurologists are now saying that the average brain contains 100 billion brain cells (neurons). Each one is like a tiny tree with messages passing from branches to roots, each making hundreds of connections to other cells as we think. The total "megabyte" capacity is inconceivably large.

LEARNING THEORY

BRAINS

BRAINS — AGING?

The myth that brain power declines with age has finally been exploded by Professor Mark Rosenzweig.

- If the brain is stimulated NO MATTER AT WHAT AGE new "twigs" will grow on each brain cell's branches and increase the total number of possible connections.

- Some of the world's most creative men have been exceptionally prolific at advanced ages (Gauguin, Michelangelo, Haydn, Picasso)

- We generate new brain connections more rapidly than the average loss of brain cells.
  EVEN IF we lose 10,000 brain cells a day from birth, the total number lost at age 80 would be less than 3%.

LEARNING THEORY

BRAINS

SPEED/PREFERENCES

Neurologists have a lot to teach teachers and trainers! Recent experiments in Brussels have shown that:

- The average person can think at 800 words per minute but the average trainer can only talk at 120 w.p.m. (so we must give our participants something interesting to do with their spare 680 w.p.m.!)

- The brain goes into "auto shut-off" after only 10 minutes if it is not given something to stimulate it (so we must vary the media and give multi-channel messages!)

- When a message is given once, the brain remembers 10% one year later. When it is given six times, recall rises to 90% (so we must repeat, recap and review)

- The brain prefers: rounded diagrams and figures to square ones; Times and Helvetica typefaces; dark letters on light background; colour, colour, colour!!!

BRAINS

RETENTION: THE PROOF

It may be that our brains retain every piece of information they ever receive ...

- ○ **DEATH-TYPE EXPERIENCES** — People snatched from death say that their entire life flashed before them ("Life after Life" Raymond Moody)

- ○ **DREAMS** — We see again "forgotten" faces and events from as many as 50 years ago

- ○ **HYPNOSIS** — Under competent supervision hypnotees have unlocked vast memory banks

- ○ **SURPRISE STIMULATION** — The 'déjà vu' experience may be triggered by sights, sounds or smells

- ○ **EXPERIMENTS** — Dr. Penfield conducted experiments where patients with electrode treatment "re-lived" past, forgotten experiences

- ○ **STORAGE** — Dr. Anokhin calculated that the storage capacity for brain cell inter-connections is the figure 1 followed by 10 million kms. of type-written zeros

- ○ **MNEMONICS** — Using special "memory systems" normal people can rival famous stage magicians

- ○ **FAMOUS EXAMPLES** — When asked what he was doing on a given day 15 years before, the famous Russian memory man called "S" asked ... "At what time ?"

LEARNING THEORY

BRAINS

RECALL: 5 MAIN FACTORS

F IRST — We are more likely to remember the beginning of events or the first in a series of events

R EVIEWED — Recall falls rapidly after 24 hours without review

O UTSTANDING — We remember unusual things exceedingly well!

L INKED — Recall is high for things which are linked by mnemonics or analogy

L AST — We are more likely to remember the end of events or the last in a series of events

(11)

LEARNING THEORY
BRAINS

RECALL

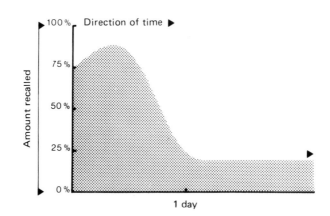

12

LEARNING THEORY

BRAINS

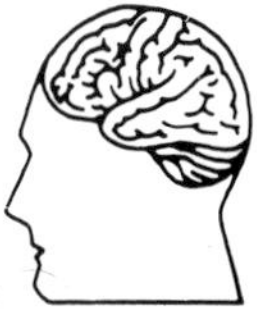

BRAINS – HOW TO KEEP RECALL HIGH

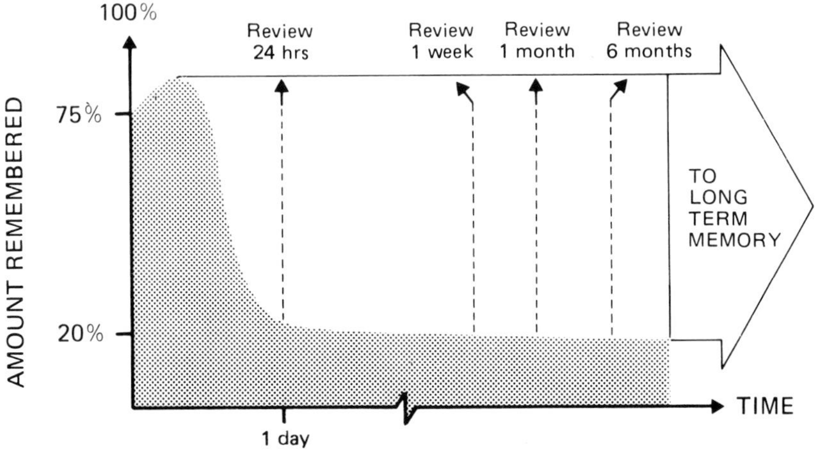

BRAINS

BRAINS — LEFT & RIGHT

- Speech
- Calculations
- Intellectual Analysis
- Reading
- Writing
- Naming
- Ordering
- Sequencing
- Complex motor sequences
- Critique
- Evaluation
- Logic

- Artistic activity
- Musical ability/Rhythm
- Emotions
- Recognition
- Comprehension
- Perception of abstract patterns
- Spatial abilities
- Facial expressions
- Holistic ability
- Intuition
- Creativity
- Images
- Colour

LEARNING THEORY

BRAINS

STIMULATING THE LEFT AND RIGHT BRAIN

Professional teachers encourage students to use both sides of the brain. Professor Robert ORNSTEIN of the University of California conducted experiments which have shown that:

- People who have been trained to use one side of the brain more than the other (Accountants, Engineers, vs. Artists, Musicians) find it difficult to "switch" when necessary

- When the weaker side is stimulated and encouraged to cooperate with the stronger side there is a great increase in ability and effectiveness (1 + 1 = 5 !)

EXAMPLE   Einstein discovered the theory of relativity while day-dreaming

APPLICATIONS   Teachers should combine analytical exercises with creative, expressive activities.

LEARNING THEORY

BRAINS

LINKING THE LEFT AND RIGHT BRAIN

Many devices exist to link the two sides of the brain and help people recall important messages. The Germans call them "donkey bridges". Creative trainers invent donkey bridges for their courses. Here are some examples you may recognise:

VISUAL ● First-letter Mnemonics (FROLL, PAMPERS, etc. See also page 11) ● Word Mnemonics (Rainbow colours = Richard Of York Gave Battle In Vain) ● Logos (Shell, Camel, Mercedes, etc) ● Composite pictures (see page 41 and donkey below!)

HEARING ● Jingles (TV Ads) ● Theme Tunes (Eurovision, etc.) ● Rhymes (30 days hath September .. etc.) ● Sounds (chalk on blackboard, gulls crying, car crashing, etc.)

FEELING ● Parables and fables (Aesop/Lafontaine) ● Examples, analogies and metaphors ("It's a bit like ..") ● Stories (e.g. to remember the planets, etc.) ● Smells (the smell of a new car) ● Tastes (the taste of your favourite food) ● Tactile "hooks" (the touch of silk, the feel of leather, etc.)

So, let's give multi-channel messages!

LEARNING THEORY

MIND SET

However hard we try to keep participant recall high, the enemy is **MIND SET.** When people hear or see something that clashes with their beliefs or values, they experience **"cognitive dissonance"** and distort or simply reject it. Here are some classic examples from the last 100 years.

- "Who the hell wants to hear actors talk?" Harry Warner, 1927

- "Sensible and responsible women do not want to vote"
  Grover Cleveland, 1927

- "Heavier-than-air flying machines are impossible" Lord Kelvin, 1895

- "There is no likelihood that man can ever tap the power of the atom"
  Robert Milikan, Nobel Prize, 1923

(17)

FURTHER READING

- "Use your Head", Tony Buzan, BBC Publications, 1974.
- "Make the Most of your Mind", Tony Buzan, Pan 1981.
- "Adults Learning", Jennifer Rogers, O.U.P., 1971.
- "Memory Matters", Mark Brown, David & Charles, 1977.
- "Left-Handed-Right-Handed", Mark Brown, David & Charles, 1979.
- "The Brain Book", Peter Russell, R.K.P., 1979.
- "Your Memory - A User's Guide", Alan Baddeley, Pelican, 1982.
- "100 Milliards de Neurones", Emile Godaux, Editions LEP, 1991

LEARNING ENVIRONMENT

LEARNING ENVIRONMENT

CHECKLIST

THE IDEAL LEARNING ENVIRONMENT
A CHECKLIST

☐ Good audio visual equipment (see appropriate section)
☐ Appropriate seating patterns
☐ Comfortable chairs
☐ Good writing surface for each student
☐ Thermostat controlled temperature
  (ideal ambient temperature = 18 °C)
☐ Independently controlled ventilation (air conditioning or windows)
☐ Good supply of coffee/light lunches
☐ Adequately sound-proofed room
☐ Natural daylight (windows with blinds/curtains)
☐ Central electrical commands (lights, A/V etc)

LEARNING ENVIRONMENT

SEATING

SEMINAR SEATING PATTERNS

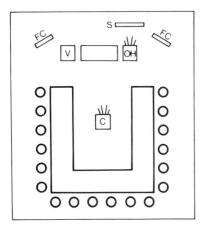

1. "U" SHAPE

Advantages

- Business-like
- Instructor can walk into "U"
- Generally good student visibility
- Standard therefore non-threatening

Disadvantages

- Somewhat formal: needs ice-breaking
- Some students masked by AV equipment
- Front students constantly at 60-90° (neck ache)
- Rear students are far from screen/FC

FC= Flip Chart / OH= Overhead / S= Screen / C= Carousel / V= Video

(21)

SEATING

SEMINAR SEATING PATTERNS

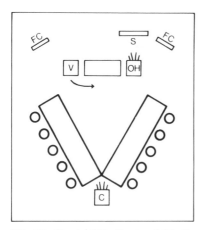

2. "V" SHAPE

Advantages

- Best pattern for visibility/neck ache
- Optimum instructor/participant contact
- Less formal and intimidating than "U"

Disadvantages

- Space requirements (only small groups)

FC= Flip Chart / OH= Overhead / S= Screen / C= Carousel / V= Video

SEMINAR SEATING PATTERNS

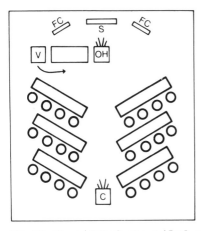

3. HERRING BONE

Advantages

- Space effective for large numbers
- All students at good angle to screen/ FC etc.
- Instructor can walk down "spine"

Disadvantages

- Several students 'masked' by others
- Reminiscent of school
- Encourages dysfunctional groupings
- Rear students far from screen/FC etc
- Relatively poor student/instructor contact

FC= Flip Chart / OH= Overhead / S= Screen / C= Carousel / V= Video

(23)

SEATING

SEMINAR SEATING PATTERNS

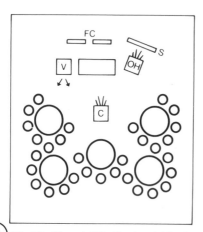

4. "BISTRO"

Advantages

- Ideal for "teambuilding" sessions and small group workshops
- Informal: encourages maximum student participation/identification
- Original: encourages open-mindedness
- Instructor can "circulate"

Disadvantages

- Some students have poor visibility or may be constantly at an angle to screen/FC
- May foster lack of attention and encourage side conversations
- Encourages splinter group identification

FC= Flip Chart / OH= Overhead / S = Screen / C = Carousel / V = Video

LEARNING ENVIRONMENT

SEATING

SEMINAR SEATING PATTERNS

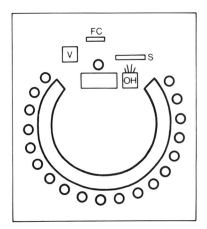

5. CIRCLE
Advantages
- Ideal for sensitivity training sessions
- Encourages maximum student involvement
- Excellent instructor student contact
- Minimum side conversations. No informal group formation

Disadvantages
- Difficult to find tables which can be set up in a circle
- Some students have poor visibility/ neck ache
- Without suitable tables students may feel unnecessarily "exposed"
- Overtones of "touchy/feely" encounter group type experience

FC= Flip Chart / OH= Overhead / S= Screen / C= Carousel / V= Video

25

SEATING

SEMINAR SEATING PATTERNS

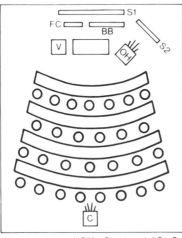

6. AMPHITHEATRE

Advantages

- If room is well designed, excellent visibility and accoustics
- Very space–effective
- Good for lecture-type presentations

Disadvantages

- Very poor instructor/student contact
- Difficult to set up unless room is designed with permanent seating
- Back rows must be elevated
- Very university-like

FC = Flip Chart / OH = Overhead / S = Screen / C = Carousel / V = Video / BB = Blackboard

SEATING

SEATING AND STUDENT PSYCHOLOGY

- Research shows that distance reduces participation
  — students in back rows are less likely to participate than those in front
- Any kind of "row" reduces interaction because of the difficulty for back rowers to hear front row contributions and for front rowers to twist round to interact with those at back
- Changes in seating patterns from one session to another can be psychologically upsetting for students
- At repetitive sessions students will invariably sit in the same place
- Angry or cynical students will attempt to move away from a group seating pattern

27

LEARNING ENVIRONMENT

MEDIA

VARYING THE MEDIA

As a general rule the learning environment should provide a change of pace / medium / subject / blood circulatory pattern every 10 minutes to avoid "auto shut-off" (see page 9).

The professional instructor will therefore plan seminar coverage so that new audio-visual interventions, and new topics come at fairly regular 10 minute intervals.

S/he will also plan for regular discussion periods, small group work or "stretch breaks" to fight the descending learning curve.

Lastly, voice control (pitch, volume, modulation) can help change the pace of a seminar.

LEARNING ENVIRONMENT

EXPERIENTIAL TEACHING

LEARNING BY DOING

Adults learn best by doing rather than listening. The ideal adult learning environment provides regular "hands-on" experiences for students to put what they have been learning into practice

EXAMPLES:
- Case studies
- Role plays
- Games and simulations
- Exercises
- Questionnaires and other instruments
- Small group discussion and reports
- Project work with presentations
- Video taped interventions with playback

SEE ALSO

PREPARING TO TEACH

PREPARING TO TEACH
QUESTIONS TO ASK

THE 5 W'S

The success of a seminar, lesson or instructional module depends on a great number of variables. Before preparing yourself to teach, you must answer 5 questions specifically — the 5 W'S!

Why?	• Ask why you are teaching at all. What are the students' objectives? What should students think or do at the end of the course?
What?	• Ask what you can put over in the available time? At what intellectual level will you pitch your teaching? What A/V aids will you need?
Who?	• Analyze the student group: Age? Nationality? Level? Language abilities? Prior experience? Expectations?
When?	• Ask whether the timing of the course is good for you and the students? Period of year? Weekdays/weekends? Morning? Afternoon? Evening?
Where?	• Ask about and prepare for environment. Building? Room? Layout? Seating patterns? Interruptions? Temperature? Noise?

STRUCTURE

HOW TO DESIGN A LEARNING EXPERIENCE

B. GUNAR EDEG R.A.F. (B)*

The Icelandic pilot who joined the
Royal Air Force (Bomber Command)

* This mnemonic device will
help you remember the 14
vital steps in designing a well
structured and memorable
learning experience.

PREPARING TO TEACH

STRUCTURE
DESIGN: STEP 1

- Always start with a learning "hook" or attention-getter.

GAP
- Establish the gap between participants' present skills/knowledge and those to be acquired during the course.

UNDERSTAND
- Check that participants understand the existence and size of skills/knowledge gap.

NEED
- Establish the need for participants to close the skills/knowledge gap.

ASK/ANSWER
- Ask and answer questions to check participants' individual needs (encourage those with smaller gap/need to help with "teaching").

RESULTS
- Outline course coverage, stressing results to be achieved (during and after the course) in closing skills/knowledge gap.

34

PREPARING TO TEACH

STRUCTURE

DESIGN: STEP 2

EXPLAIN
- Explain each new skill/learning in digestible chunks using appropriate Visual, Hearing & Feeling support. (see page **85**)

DEMONSTRATE
- Demonstrate skills and/or show how knowledge applies to them. Use VHF support.

EXERCISE
- Allow participants to exercise each new skill or to feedback their understanding of new knowledge.

GUIDE/CORRECT
- Show participants how well they have learned and correct any inadequacies.

STRUCTURE

DESIGN: STEP 3

Recap
- Review all learning points at end of each module (or beginning of next). Use VHF support.

Action plan
- Agree on an action plan for the transfer of new skills or knowlege to real life.

Follow-up
- Agree on any follow-up or refresher.

Bang!
- Always finish with a succinct and provocative encapsulation of the learning experience.

36

NOTES

LECTURE/SEMINAR INSTRUCTOR NOTES

Dr Gordon Howe of Exeter University, UK, conducted a study on the effectiveness of various forms of lecture notes used by university teachers in terms of instructor recall, self-confidence and material coverage as well as student attention and interest. He ranked the different kinds of notes from 1 (high) to 7 (low)

1. Key words prepared by lecturer
2. Key words copied from source documents
3. Summary sentences prepared by lecturer
4. Summary sentences copied from source documents
5. Transcript written by lecturer
6. Transcript of original source documents
7. No notes !

KEY WORDS

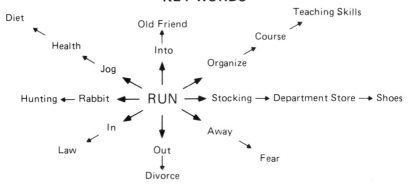

"A key creative word sprays out associations in all directions ... it funnels itself into a wide range of images and, when triggered, funnels back the same images"   Tony Buzan "Use your Head" BBC 1974

NOTES

MIND MAP

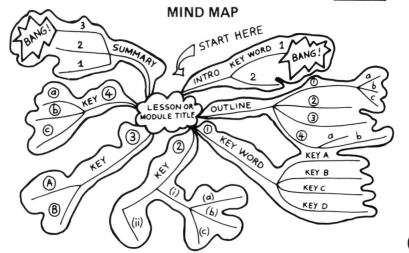

MIND MAP EXERCISE

PREPARING TO TEACH

MEMORY TECHNIQUES

IMAGES

Instant recall of complicated concepts or lists of items to be taught can be helped by making unusual mental pictures

EXAMPLE:

Imagine you have to remember to get your child from school, shop for wine and bananas and ring your friends. Make a mental image like the one opposite, anchor it as "things to do" and — you'll do them!

MEMORY TECHNIQUES

MNEMONICS
"Device for improving the memory"

The most common and useful mnemonic for the professional trainer is to take the first letter of a list of points to remember and make a memory-jogging new word or phrase

EXAMPLES:

E very
G ood
B oy
D eserves
F avours

Maslow's Hierarchy of Needs

S tamped **A** ddressed
E nvelope to
B ernard
S haw's
P ussycat

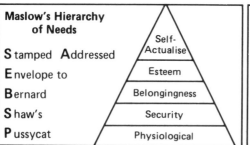

- Self-Actualise
- Esteem
- Belongingness
- Security
- Physiological

Socratic Direction

K now the answers you want
O pen questioning
P araphrase answers
S ummarize contributions
A dd your own comment

42

MEMORY TECHNIQUES

NAMES AND FACES

Whenever faced with a class of new students whose names you want and need to remember:

- Listen to name
- Spell it in your head
- Repeat name as often as possible in class
- Look for an outstanding facial feature
- Exaggerate the feature
- Associate   — Mrs. Hawkes   = Beaked nose
           — Mr. White   = Sickness/fear/clown
           — Mr. Metropoulos   = Big town, city slicker

MEMORY TECHNIQUES

NAME CARDS

Unless you are in a formal school setting make sure that each student is provided with a ready-made or do-it-yourself "tent card" for his/her name. Ask for big bold letters so you can read the name from any part of the teaching area

PREPARING TO TEACH

SEMINAR TIMING

DOWN TIME

In a seminar day of 9 hours
(08.30–17.30) always plan for
down time as follows:

- Latecomers, settling, housekeeping
  = 10 mins

- Coffee/Tea breaks
  = 20 + 20 = 40 mins (even if you
  have planned 15 minute breaks!)

- Lunch and "re-settling" after lunch
  = 75 mins (even if you have planned
  1 hour!)

- Stretch breaks, breaking into
  syndicates and other miscellaneous
  down time = 25 mins

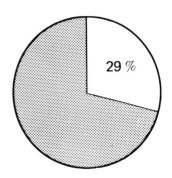

29 %

Total = 2 hrs 30

SEMINAR TIMING

TIMING TIPS

- Always keep a clock or watch on your desk
  — but don't rely on looking at the watch on your wrist

- Use a chronometer or good kitchen timer for timing break-out sessions, separate modules etc.

- Always allow time for discussion — build it in to your course plan

PREPARING TO TEACH

TRAINING METHODS

EFFECTIVENESS OF DIFFERENT TRAINING METHODS

METHOD	Ranking of methods depending on TEACHING GOALS (1 = high, 8 = low)					
	Knowledge acquisition	Attitude change	Problem-solving skills	Inter-personal skills	Participant acceptance	Knowledge retention
CASE STUDY	4	5	1	5	1	4
WORKSHOP	1	3	4	4	5	2
LECTURE	8	7	7	8	7	3
GAMES	5	4	2	3	2	7
FILMS	6	6	8	6	4	5
PROGRAMMED INST	3	8	6	7	8	1
ROLE-PLAYING	2	2	3	1	3	6
'T' GROUP	7	1	5	2	6	8

Source : "Evaluating the Effectiveness of Training Methods" — J. Newstrom. Personnel Administration. January 1980

PREPARING TO TEACH

TRAINER PREPARATION

HOW TO BEAT MURPHY!

- Always carry a checklist of material, equipment, etc. to the training site.
- Arrive at the training site at least one hour before the start of the programme to prepare material and equipment.
- Take at least 15 minutes from this time to prepare yourself:
  · physically - centering energy, grooming, posture and breathing
  · mentally - visualising the participant group, trying to imagine how they are feeling and asking/answering the question, "How can I best HELP these people to change and grow, given the programme objectives and organisational culture?"
- Consciously manage personal energy levels by avoiding temptations to over-eat, over-drink or under-sleep before or during the programme.
- Keep physically fit with at least one type of exercise per week.

Based on Team Training International's "Professional Standards for Trainers" 1993

48

PLATFORM SKILLS

ANALYZING THE STUDENT GROUP

GETTING TO KNOW THEM

- Always begin with an "ice breaker" (see Exercises)
- Get students talking as soon as possible
- Watch non-verbal behaviour*
- Encourage the quiet ones to contribute*
- Don't allow eager beavers to dominate*
- Find out each student's level, position and background as soon as possible
- Have a participants list — make notes

* See pages on discussion leading

ENTHUSIASM

YOU GOTTA BELIEVE !

- If you're not enthusiastic about your subject, how can you expect the students to be !!
- Consciously use your eyes and eyebrows to communicate enthusiasm
- Always keep a sparkle in your voice
- Fight boredom of repetitive sessions by introducing new anecdotes, examples etc or by changing lesson structure

DISCUSSION LEADING

"B" ING

Here are 4 ways to keep a class discussion going:

- **BUILDING** — Build on incomplete answers by adding own comments and asking for agreement or disagreement.

- **BOOSTING** — Support timid participants' contributions, boost their confidence and ask for extra comment.

- **BLOCKING** — Interrupt dominant/talkative/ aggressive participants by asking what others think.

- **BANTERING** — Establish non-threatening atmosphere by engaging in friendly repartee with outgoing participants.

DISCUSSION LEADING

BRAINSTORMING

A technique for obtaining ideas from a group. Here's how:

Ask   Ask for/provoke ideas. If necessary wait 45 seconds before giving own.

Record   Write **ALL** ideas on a flip chart (number them for future reference). Don't evaluate 'til end.

Trigger   Use ''B''ing discussion leading techniques to encourage participants to trigger ideas.

Summarize   Summarize and/or regroup ideas. Help group to choose best.

(53)

DISCUSSION LEADING

SOCRATIC DIRECTION

Take a tip from the Ancient Greeks.

If you wish to encourage audience participation to prove a point use SOCRATIC DIRECTION

K now the answers you want

O pen questioning technique

P araphrase participants' answers

S ummarize contributions (flip chart?)

A dd your own points

DISCUSSION LEADING

CLASS CONTROL

● REGULATING	Interrupt long-winded talkers with questions. Bring red-herring posers back to subject. Use directive techniques where necessary
● FOCUSSING	Keep the current topic in front of class. Use A/V equipment to refocus attention. Ask closed questions
● GUIDING	Ask reflective questions. Use socratic direction. Give examples of what **you** want to get across
● INTERPRETING	Interpret or paraphrase badly thought-out contributions. Rephrase remarks which arouse class antagonism. Refocus when questions lead away from subject
● SUMMARIZING	Give overview and recap points covered at every logical and/or convenient point

DISCUSSION LEADING

TEACHING TEMPO

2 factors will govern the tempo of your material coverage and discussion periods:

1. The students' level of knowledge and general intelligence

- low = slow
- high = fast

2. Your own teaching style

- snappy/authoritarian/directive = fast
- relaxed, informal, facilitative = slow

How to change tempo

- SLOWER — Use more cases, examples, anecdotes. Speak slower. Ask open questions
- FASTER — Speak faster. Use more directive tone. Cut down discussions. Ask closed questions

DISCUSSION LEADING

METHODS FOR DEALING WITH STUDENT QUESTIONS OR STATEMENTS

- **STRAIGHTFORWARD** . . . . .Answer the question
- **OVERHEAD** . . . .''Good question. What are some of the other questions we should also ask about. . . . . ?''
- **RELAY**. . . . .''Thanks for the question. Have some of you others met the same problem ?''
- **RICOCHET** . . . . .Good point ! Bill; you had something to say on this one earlier . . . . . ?''
- **REVERSE**. . . . . .When the question is really a statement, hand the answering back to the poser.
- **STATEMENT ?**. . . . .''What point are we discussing now ?'' (i.e. we're wandering)

   STATEMENT !. . . . .''I think we should come back to this point later''

PLATFORM SKILLS

DISCUSSION LEADING

QUESTIONING SKILLS

CLOSED QUESTIONS — Who can tell me on which date ?
                              — Which/what specifically ?

OPEN QUESTIONS

- "About" — How do you feel about ... ?
- Reflective — You don't feel comfortable with ... ?
- Hypothetical — What do you think would happen if ... ?
- Framing — Help me to see how this fits with ... ?
- Silence — .... ?
- Statements — Rosemary, you look as it you wanted to say something

ALWAYS AVOID: Multiple — a string of questions
                   Leading — "Don't you think it would be better to ... ?"

58

DISCUSSION LEADING

LUBRICATORS

Verbal

- "I see"
- "Ah, ah"
- "That's interesting !"
- "Really ?"
- "Go on !"
- "Tell me more about that"

Non-Verbal

- Nodding
- Constant eye contact
- Leaning forward
- Stepping aside
- Raising eyebrows
- Frowning
  (encourages clarification)

QUESTIONS & INTERRUPTIONS

Most participant questions are not questions. They are requests for the spotlight. If it's one of those rare, closed REAL questions — answer it succinctly. If not, first:

- **REFLECT**   back to the questioner what you thought was the question. ("If I understand correctly, you're asking ....")

Depending on how the questioner "reformulates" the question, answer it OR:

- **DEFLECT**   it as follows:

  - **GROUP** : "How do the rest of the group feel?"
    : "Has anyone else had a similar problem?"
  - **RICOCHET** : (to one participant) "Bill, you're an expert on this?"
  - **REVERSE** : (back to questioner) "You've obviously done some thinking on this. What's **your** view?"

PLATFORM SKILLS

DEALING WITH DIFFICULT PARTICIPANTS

1. THE HECKLER :

- Probably insecure
- Gets satisfaction from needling
- Aggressive and argumentative

What to do :

- Never get upset
- Find merit, express agreement, move on
- Wait for a mis-statement fact and then throw it out to the group for correction

DEALING WITH DIFFICULT PARTICIPANTS

2. THE TALKER/KNOW ALL
- An "eager beaver"/chatterbox
- A show-off
- Well-informed and anxious to show it

What to do:

- Wait 'til he/she takes a breath, thank, refocus and move on
- Slow him/her down with a tough question
- Jump in and ask for group to comment

DEALING WITH DIFFICULT PARTICIPANTS

3. THE GRIPER

- Feels "hard done by"
- Probably has a pet "peeve"
- Will use you as scapegoat

What to do:

- Get him/her to be specific
- Show that the purpose of your presentation is to be positive and constructive
- Use peer pressure

DEALING WITH DIFFICULT PARTICIPANTS

4. THE WHISPERERS
   (There's only one.
   The other is the
   "whisperee"!)

- Don't understand what's going on — clarifying or translating
- Sharing anecdotes triggered by your presentation
- Bored, mischievous or hypo-critical (unusual)

What to do:

- Stop talking, wait for them to look up and "non-verbally" ask for their permission to continue

- Use "lighthouse" technique

DEALING WITH DIFFICULT PARTICIPANTS

5. THE SILENT ONE
- Timid, insecure, shy
- Bored, indifferent

What to do:

- Timid?

  Ask easy question. Boost his/her ego in discussing answer. Refer to by name when giving examples. Bolster confidence.

- Bored?

  Ask tough questions. Refer to by name as someone who ''surely knows that...'' Use as helper in exercises.

DEALING WITH DIFFICULT PARTICIPANTS

PSYCHOLOGICAL JUDO
(when classical methods have not worked!)

In physical judo you use the energy of your opponent to cause his downfall by changing your "push" into "pull". In psychological judo you ask the difficult participants to be **even more** difficult. This gives them even more of the spotlight and attention than they wanted and they will use their energy to "pull back" to avoid ridicule or overkill.

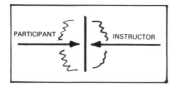

CLASSICAL CONFRONTATION

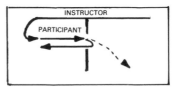

PSYCHOLOGICAL JUDO

● See page 68 for examples

PLATFORM SKILLS

DEALING WITH DIFFICULT PARTICIPANTS

PSYCHOLOGICAL JUDO

The Pipe Smoker

In order to illustrate Psychological Judo let's take a difficult participant
— the inveterate, pungently obnoxious pipe smoker.
Instead of asking him to refrain from smoking in class you give him a
whistle and, having commiserated with him about the intolerance of
non-smokers, ask him to blow the whistle hard and loud when he
thinks you should stop the class for a smoke break.
It takes a brave smoker to exercise the right! When he blows the
whistle he is really saying "I'm a drug addict". In fact he'll use his
energy to "prove" he can hold out 'til coffee break!!

DEALING WITH DIFFICULT PARTICIPANTS

PSYCHOLOGICAL JUDO – EXAMPLES

1. THE HECKLER — Appoint as class "devil's advocate". Insist that s/he criticise **whenever** s/he feels you are leading class astray. Demand negative remarks.

2. THE KNOW-ALL — Agree with and amplify "know-all" contributions. Ask for expert judgement when none is forthcoming. Get him/her up front to teach short module. Refer constantly to their expertise in subject matter taught.

3. THE GRIPER — Ask for written list of gripes to help class maintain sense of realism. Get him/her to read list at end of day. Add to list whenever possible!

4. THE WHISPERERS — State that time is short and ask those who don't understand not to interrupt but to ask their neighbour!

5. THE SILENT ONE — State that some people are shy and dare not participate. This does not mean they have not understood. Encourage shy ones **NOT** to participate.

PLATFORM SKILLS
USING YOUR VOICE

Ⓟ ROJECTION — Speak louder than usual. Throw your voice to back of room

Ⓐ RTICULATION — Don't swallow words. Beware of verbal "tics"

Ⓜ ODULATION — Vary tone and pitch. Be dramatic, confidential and/or triumphant

Ⓟ RONUNCIATION — Watch tonic accents. Check difficult words. Beware of malapropisms

Ⓔ NUNCIATION — Over emphasize. Accentuate syllables

Ⓡ EPETITION — Repeat key phrases with different vocal emphasis

Ⓢ PEED — Use delivery speed to manipulate the audience! Fast delivery to excite and stimulate. Slow delivery to emphasize, awe, dramatize and control.

69

MANNERISMS

- Don't be tempted by manual props (pens, pointers, spectacles etc.)
- Don't keep loose change in your pocket
- Be aware of your verbal tics and work on eliminating them (i.e. "OK!" – "You know" – "and so forth" – "Now ...")
- Don't smoke (unless seated in discussion mode)
- Watch out for furniture!
- Avoid "closed" or tense body positions
- Don't worry about pacing, leaning etc.
- Check your hair/tie/trousers/dress before standing up!

LIGHTHOUSE TECHNIQUE

Sweep the audience with your eyes, staying only 2-3 seconds on each person - unless in dialogue.

This will give each participant the impression that you are speaking to him/her personally and ensure attention, in the same way as the lighthouse keeps you awake by its regular sweeping flash of light. Above all, avoid looking at one (friendly-looking) member of the audience or at a fixed (non-threatening) point on the wall or floor.

PLATFORM SKILLS
NERVES: THE MURPHY MONKEY

As you get up to speak, it's as if a monkey has suddenly jumped onto your shoulders. He claws your neck and weighs you down - making your knees feel weak and shaky. As you start to speak, he pulls at your vocal chords and dries up your saliva. He pushes your eyes to the floor, makes your arms feel 10 metres long and attaches a piece of elastic to your belt - pulling you back to the table or wall behind you !

Experienced speakers know about the Murphy monkey. Within the first 30 seconds they throw him to the audience ! When you throw the monkey to one of the participants, suddenly the spotlight is on them and not on you. How...?

● A question, a show of hands, a short "icebreaker" (participant introductions, an exercise or quiz etc.) a discussion, a "volunteer" or simply a reference to one or more of the participants - all these are ways of putting the monkey on **their** backs for a few moments.

This takes the pressure off you and gives you time to relax, smile and get ready to communicate your message loud and clear.

PLATFORM SKILLS

SENSITIVITY & TACT

PREVENT FOOT-IN-MOUTH DISEASE !

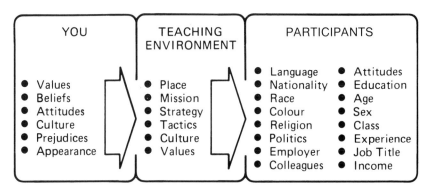

YOU	TEACHING ENVIRONMENT	PARTICIPANTS	
● Values	● Place	● Language	● Attitudes
● Beliefs	● Mission	● Nationality	● Education
● Attitudes	● Strategy	● Race	● Age
● Culture	● Tactics	● Colour	● Sex
● Prejudices	● Culture	● Religion	● Class
● Appearance	● Values	● Politics	● Experience
		● Employer	● Job Title
		● Colleagues	● Income

BE AWARE — BEWARE !

73

PLATFORM SKILLS

DRESS

- Avoid black and white and other strongly contrasting colours

- Wear comfortable, loose-fitting clothes

- If you can't make up your mind, wear something boring - at least your clothes won't detract from the message !

- Try and dress one step above the audience

- Check zips and buttons before standing up

When in doubt, a blue blazer, grey slacks and black shoes with a white shirt and striped tie is usually acceptable from the board room to the art studio.

PLATFORM SKILLS
TEN TIPS

- ❏ Don't keep your eyes on your notes
- ❏ Never read anything except quotations
- ❏ If you're not nervous there's something wrong

The day I lose my stage-fright is the day I stop acting
Sir Laurence Olivier

- ❏ Exaggerate body movements and verbal emphasis
- ❏ **PERFORM** (don't act) Perform = "fournir" (to supply) and "per" (for)
- ❏ Pause often - silence is much longer for **you** than for the audience
- ❏ Use humour. A laugh is worth a thousand frowns !
- ❏ Be enthusiastic. If you're not, why should they be ?
- ❏ Don't try and win the Nobel prize for technical accuracy
- ❏ **KISS**. **K**eep **I**t **S**imple, **S**tupid !

YOU CAN'T **NOT** COMMUNICATE

Research has shown that when someone gives a spoken message the listener's understanding and judgement of that message comes from:

7% WORDS
- Words are only labels and listeners put their own interpretation on speakers' words.

38% PARALINGUISTICS
- The **way** in which something is said (i.e. accent, tone, inflection etc.) is very important to a listener's understanding.

55% FACIAL EXPRESSIONS
- What a speaker looks like while delivering a message affects the listener's understanding most.

• RESEARCH SOURCE – ALBERT MEHRABIAN

PLATFORM SKILLS

LISTENING

ACTIVE LISTENING

Whenever a participant interrupts or responds emotionally during a lesson s/he is probably overstating his or her feelings in order to justify the "outburst". In **every** such case use Active Listening. Never attempt to counter, argue, defend or take sides.

1. Take the outburst as a positive contribution (smile, encourage, nod, use lubricators)
2. Successively reflect back to the participant (in the form of questions) what feelings you heard being expressed. "You're upset with ...?" "You're unhappy about...?" "You feel that we should...?"

Active Listening has 3 advantages:

- You show the participant you're interested and not defensive
- You allow the participant to confirm that what you heard was what s/he meant OR to correct your interpretation
- You quickly lead the participant to specify the EXACT problem and to suggest a solution

77

TYPES OF BODY LANGUAGE

Postures & Gestures

- How do you use hand gestures? Sitting position? Stance?

Eye Contact

- How's your "Lighthouse"?!

Orientation

- How do you position yourself in class?

Proximity

- How close do you sit/stand to participants?

Looks/Appearance

- Are looks/appearance/dress important?

Expressions of Emotion

- Are you using facial expressions to express emotion?

POSTURES AND GESTURES: HANDS

STEEPLING

- Self Confidence (Intellectual Arrogance?)

HAND CLASP

- Anxious, controlled

NOSE TOUCH

- Doubt

"L" CHIN REST

- Critical Evaluation

MOUTH BLOCK

- Resisting speech

79

POSTURES AND GESTURES: SITTING

ARMS UP
- Reserved, defensive

ARM/LEG CROSS
- Closed, unconvinced

LEAN FORWARD
- Ready!

LEAN BACK
- Confident superiority

LINT-PICKING
- Disapproval

POSTURES AND GESTURES: STANDING

THUMBS OUT

- In charge! Dominant

FIG LEAF

- Self-control, tense

ARMS OUT PALMS UP

- Open, sincere, conciliatory

TABLE LEAN

- Authoritative, involved

LEAN ON

- Unthreatened, casual belongingness

81

FURTHER READING/LISTENING

- "Tips for Trainers", John Townsend, 1992. Audio Cassette available from Management Pocketbooks (see Order Form).

- "Professional Standards for Trainers", Team Training Int., 1993. TTI, Isbarrygasse 12, A-1140 Wien, Austria.

- "Silent Messages", Albert Mehrabian, 1981, Wadsworth Inc.

- "Bodily Communication", Michael Argyle, 1988, Methuen.

- "Manwatching", Desmond Morris, Jonathan Cape.

AUDIO/VISUAL AIDS

PRESENTATIONS KIT

MASKING TAPE

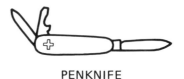

PENKNIFE

 x 3 colours

MARKERS

Professional Instructors always carry this emergency kit

84

VHF COMMUNICATION

Human beings store incoming data in one of 3 ways:

Visual: they memorize pictures, images, diagrams, charts, graphs etc.

Hearing: they memorize sounds, conversations, melodies, accents etc.

Feeling: they memorize emotions, smells, tastes, tactile experiences and . . . pain.

However, each of us has a preferred "channel" for remembering data (V, H or F). So, the good speaker provides his varied audience with as wide a range of stimuli as possible. Here's a resumé of the aids and techniques available to you:

Visual Aids ● Flip Chart ● Black/White/Pin Board ● Overhead Projector ● Slide Projector ● Props ● Video Clips ● Word Pictures*

Hearing Aids ● Audio cassettes ● Video ● Sound effects ● Music ● Onomatopoeia*

Feeling Aids ● Music ● Handouts ● Props ● Verbal description/analogies*
Remember: Feelings stay longer than facts.

*Yes, if you don't have the equipment − use your voice!

(85)

FLIP TIPS

PREPARATION

INVISIBLE OUTLINE

Lightly pencil in headings in advance when unsure of space, drawing, handwriting etc.

CORNER CRIB

Use the top corner to pencil in your notes for each chart. Write small and no one will notice!

READY-MADE

Prepare key charts in advance

PAPER

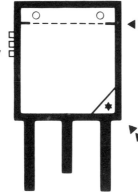

When you know you will want
to tear off a sheet to display on
wall, score top with a ruler and
cut first few milimeters each
side to ensure a smooth tear

Tab sections with
headings for easy
reference

Cut corners off preceding sheets
when you need quick access to
a particular page

FLIP TIPS

GRAPHICS

- Write more clearly and use BIGGER letters than you think you have to.

- SPACE out ideas.

- USE DARK COLOURS (Beware of yellow, light red and light green).

- Never leave material on flip chart which is no longer relevant. When in doubt — FLIP!

GRAPHICS

Whenever possible use cartoons or drawings to personalize and add interest to your headings

GRAPHICS

STANDING

Every time you turn your back on the audience your voice and their attention disappear.

Since you can't write AND face the audience at the same time (unless you are a contortionist!) you should:

- Write (a few words/seconds)
- Turn and Talk
- Write (a few words/seconds)
- Turn and Talk . . . .

THE WHITEBOARD

WRITING AND STICKING

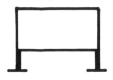

WRITE ON!

- Replaces blackboard (school memories)
- Great for "mind map" summaries/brainstorming (see pages 39 & 53)
- Change colour often
- Only use appropriate whiteboard pens

STICK UP!

- Use 3M "Post-it" stickers to create group-work summaries (key phrases only). Stick on whiteboard
- Move stickers into columns or categories. Use pens to draw bubbles round salient groupings or to make links between stickers.

THE PINWAND

PINWALL WIZARD

The lightweight, collapsible pinwand (pin wall) is the ideal visual aid for facilitators and project leaders.

WRITING — Cover pinwand surface with large sheet of brown paper (from same supplier). Use as flip chart.

PINNING — Distribute coloured cards (same supplier) for exercises/group work. Collect and pin to board in categories. Add headings, illustrations etc.

STICKING — Cover pinwand with large sheet, spray with contact glue. Stick cards/cut outs as above.

GRAPHICS

WHEN YOU KNOW
WHAT YOU WANT
TO
WRITE, ALWAYS

PLAN AHEAD

THE PROJECTOR

- Make sure the projector lens and projection surface are clean before starting your presentation
  (If you can't get hold of some glass cleaning liquid and a cloth, turn the projector off and use a handkerchief and "spit and polish")

- Check for a spare projector lamp

- Test projector/screen distance with a sample transparency for positioning and focus

94

SCREEN POSITION

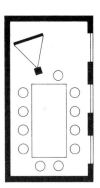

- The best position for the screen is in a corner of the conference room — high enough for everyone to see without craning, peeping, standing or !eaning!

O/H PROJECTOR RULES

PROJECTION ANGLE

- Avoiding the "Keystone" effect

  Keep the projector beam at 90° to the screen by tilting the screen (ideal) or by jacking up the projector until keystone disappears. If you jack the projector you'll need a chock to prevent transparencies sliding forward.

PROJECTOR POSITIONING

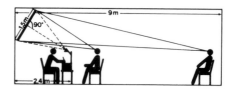

PLANNING A SERIES
OF TRANSPARENCIES

- Create transparencies which are simple, concise and expressive

- Project images designed to catch attention:
  - SURPRISE
  - REASONING
  - QUESTIONING
  - SUSPENSE
  - HUMOUR

- Emphasize only major points of your message

- Illustrate only ONE topic per transparency
  (If necessary use the Revelation or Overlay technique)

- Limit message to 6-8 lines of 6 words each

GOLDEN RULES

FRAME
Use a standard, HORIZONTAL frame & "Logo" (like this page!) for all transparencies

LARGE
USE LARGE, LEGIBLE LETTERS
Titles = 2 cm. Text = 1 cm.

IMAGES
Use illustrations on ALL transparencies

COLOUR
Use 2-3 complementary colours on ALL transparencies

KISS
Keep it simple, stupid! One idea only per transparency

PRODUCING TRANSPARENCIES

Professional Production

- High Quality (letters, colours, design)
- Expensive ($60-$200 per transparency)

Do-it-yourself

- Print or stick graphics and text from computer software (or produce freehand artwork) onto horizontal, framed A4 original.

- Photo-copy or laser print directly onto transparency

or: - Photo-copy onto paper then use a thermo copier (flexible — lighter/darker copies)

SPECIAL TIPS ▶ Use outline letters and colour in later. Never use typed text (too small: see page 42).

(see page 42)

(99)

PRODUCING TRANSPARENCIES

Computer Generated
A whole range of software exists for P.C. generated lettering and graphics (i.e. HP Draw, DEC Prosight). Although costly and time-consuming the result is a crisp and colourful slide.
Transparencies are generated either by photographing the P.C. screen or directly via plotter onto the acetate.

Mechanical
- The "Brother P. Touch" stamps out text on a transparent tape in a selection of type faces
- Transfer letters from Letraset or Mecanorma can be pressed onto original artwork letter by letter.

PRODUCING TRANSPARENCIES

FREEHAND LETTERING

- Use Permanent O/H pens
- Place transparency on squared paper to ensure allignment
- Use colour as much as possible
- Be bold! Practise your own "alphabet"
- For full letters, use light colour to block in letters before out-lining with darker colour

PRODUCING TRANSPARENCIES

SYMBOLS

- Wherever possible use symbols as well as letters.
  Don't be afraid to use "speech bubbles", large arrows or "special offer" flashes:

O/H PRESENTATIONS KIT

REVELATION
MASK

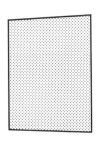

TRANSPARENCY SLEEVE OR
FLIP FRAME BINDER

O/H COLOURED PEN SET
(MEDIUM: PERMANENT)

103

PRESENTATION TECHNIQUES

WITH PLASTIC FRAME (Staedler)

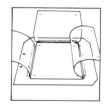

OVERLAY

- Use several superimposed transparencies to build up a story or argument

  NB Make sure you mount your overlays so that they fit onto each other exactly — everytime

WITH CARD FRAME (3M)

PRESENTATION TECHNIQUES

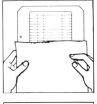

REVELATION

◀ ● When you have several important points on one transparency, use a mask to gradually reveal your argument step by step.
(If you don't, your audience will be reading point 6 when you're talking about point 1)

◀ ● For important, high quality presentation, try the "window" technique

(105)

PRESENTATION TECHNIQUES

ANIMATION

- Solid objects or cut-outs on the projection surface will block the light and give sharp silhouettes on the screen
  With cardboard cut-outs you can design an interesting and original animated presentation

EXAMPLE:

Production process, moving arrow.
Female silhouette, light bulb etc.

SPECIAL TIP ▶ Could be a good opening BANG!

THE CASSETTE RECORDER/PLAYER

MUSIC

Here are some ways you should be using recorded music in your training seminars:

- To create a friendly atmosphere at the beginning of the course as participants come in, meet each other and settle down.
- As background music during coffee breaks/intervals.
- To provide a relaxed "learning" environment during exercises; tests, etc.
- As an introductory "bang".
- To create specific atmospheres for special messages (film music, theme tunes, sound effects, etc.).
- To illustrate a point amusingly with a song "snippet" (Example for a course on Customer Service: "Help", "Keep the customer satisfied", "You can't always get what you want", etc.).

THE CASSETTE RECORDER/PLAYER

VOICE

Recorded speech can be useful for :

- Illustrating role-plays (Interviewing, Public Speaking, Salesman-Customer, Boss-Subordinate)
- Examples of opinions (market research interviews etc.)
- Bringing an absent colleague to the seminar
- Interjecting humorous anecdotes
- Giving examples of current radio ads/trends
- Use a cassette deck to record your presentation so you can work on your mistakes

   NB   When recording audio examples make sure you leave very little space between each recording. In this way you can press the "pause" button at the end of one example knowing that the next recording is cued to start as soon as you next hit the button.

WHEN TO USE PHOTOGRAPHIC SLIDES?

- When you have the time and the money!

- When you need a "higher quality" presentation

- When you want to show photographs/cartoons etc.

- When you wish to change pace or differentiate from colleagues' omnipresent overhead slides

- When you wish to dramatize a point and create expectancy by darkening the conference room

- When contact with and participation of the audience is not essential

WHEN NOT TO USE PHOTOGRAPHIC SLIDES

- When you only have words to show
- When you can't darken the room sufficiently
- When audience participation is important
- When you are a persuasive ''eye contact'' speaker
- When you have a tight budget!
- When ''everybody else does, so I suppose ...''
- When you don't know how to work the projector

PHOTOGRAPHIC SLIDES
THE MISSING LINK

Many slide presentations fail because they forget that slides should be used as VISUALS. Examples of where slides can be used to clarify things visually are:

- Charts and Graphs — instead of tables
- Diagrams of processes — instead of words
- Photographs — instead of descriptions
- Flow charts — instead of lists
- Graphic Titles (Logos, Drawings etc.)
- Cartoons — instead of anecdotes

PHOTOGRAPHIC SLIDES
SLIDE RULES

Make sure the agency/friend who does your slides will:

- Always use several colours
- Be aware and beware of ''colour camouflage''
  (i.e. no yellow on white, blue on green, pink on red etc.)
- Never put more than 6 lines of max. 6 words
  (Ideal = what you could write on a T-shirt)
- Use photos, cartoons, drawings as much as possible
- Use a consistent design for series of slides
- Keep words horizontal (especially on pie charts)
- Never show photos of pages from a book
- Remember that words are not visual aids!

16 mm AND VIDEO FILMS
QUESTIONS

- Does the film really support your message?

- Does the film raise questions which you'd rather avoid?

- Is the occasion right?
  - a budget presentation — probably not
  - a sales training meeting — maybe

- Can you work the projector/video player?

- Is it too complicated to set up?

- Can you afford the time for necessary discussion?

- Can you risk people falling asleep?

APPLICATIONS

TRAINING

- Video is the best teacher in interpersonal skills training:

  "I am what others tell me I am" becomes: "I am what I see I am"

IMPROVING TEAMWORK

- When you record a group session on video:

  "I understand what my behaviour does to you because you, or another group member tells me", becomes: "I understand what my behaviour does to you because I see it"

GROUP & INDIVIDUAL EXERCISES

GROUP & INDIVIDUAL EXERCISES

ICEBREAKERS

Some ideas for introduction exercises to break the ice at the beginning of a lesson, course or seminar:

●	AUTOGRAPHS	Ask students to circulate and obtain signatures of others students on a list of statements i.e. "Drives a sport car"
●	BUSINESS CARD	Give students 3 minutes to devise their "dream" business card — a fictitious name and job title which they would like to have. Go round the table discussing each "dream".
●	DYAD INTRODUCTIONS	Ask each student to "interview" his neighbour for 5 minutes and then present the neighbour to the rest of the class
●	MAP	Draw a rough map of the country (world/continent/region). Hang the map in front of the class and ask each student in turn to come up and mark his/her home town on the map, giving a one minute description of the town

GROUP & INDIVIDUAL EXERCISES

THE QUIZ

In training courses where facts must be learned it is essential to "exercise" students' new knowledge. Written tests are fine but remind students of their school days.
A well-devised quiz will appeal and test at the same time.

SUGGESTIONS
- Break group into quiz teams to provoke competition
- Invent different categories of questions like on T.V. game shows
- Keep scores on imaginatively designed board (Whiteboard/Pinwand)
- Don't forget the prizes!

CASE STUDIES

CASE STUDIES

Concisely written, practical and realistic case studies will induce thinking, analysis, pro and con discussion and genuine efforts to find solutions to problems. Case studies help students to apply theoretical knowledge to real-life situations and also serve as "pace-changers" to stimulate interest and attention

Case Study Rules for Instructors

- Know the facts of case study well
- Have pre-prepared questions to guide students during their own analysis of the facts
- Tabulate consensus items during discussion
- Encourage differences of opinion to explore alternative solutions
- The instructor should use Socratic Direction (see page 54) to finalize learnings from the case study

ROLE-PLAYING 1

ROLE-PLAYING

Role-playing is a dramatized form of case study in which students act out a human relations problem situation under the guidance of the instructor who elicits an evaluation of the performance in light of previously taught principles

PREREQUISITES FOR A SUCCESSFUL ROLE-PLAYING EXERCISE:

- The role play situation must be realistic
- The situation must be one with which students can identify. Characters should be of a type that really exist in the organization
- Students must live their parts
- Role-playing should not represent a threat to timid students
- Instructor should play the "challenger" role.

ROLE-PLAYING IS NOT PLAY ACTING. IT IS "REALITY PRACTICE"

GROUP & INDIVIDUAL EXERCISES

ROLE-PLAYING FEEDBACK RULES

1. First ask role-player(s) for an "auto-critique"
2. Ask group to take notes and watch the video re-play
(where appropriate)
3. Ask the group to give feedback

RULES

- Always separate "motivational" from "developmental" feedback
- For developmental feedback, use the conditional tense and always offer an alternative (i.e. "I think it would have been more effective if you had ...")
- Always address the individual concerned and say "you" not "he/she"

GROUP & INDIVIDUAL EXERCISES

PROJECT WORK

PROJECTS

In courses and seminars which are constructed in modules given at regular weekly/monthly etc. intervals project work between sessions provides an ideal bridging learning and review experience.

1. Tailor-made   As an instructor you should develop relevant project structures which will allow students to practise each session's learning points — if possible in groups of 4-7

2. Canned   Many video-based packages exist which provide inter-session project work as an integral part of the course
(see "The Penguin Video Source Book", 1983)

PROJECT WORK

THE GROUP RECAP

One kind of project which is worth highlighting is the group recap.

In courses which last more than one day you split the group into small teams and ask a different team to make a resumé of the previous day's learning at the start of each new day.

Teams invariably vie with one another to make **their** resumé the best (at least the most amusing), a lot of learning takes place and a good time is had by all (especially the instructor who has one less module to teach!)

GROUP & INDIVIDUAL EXERCISES

INSTRUMENTS

SEMINAR INSTRUMENTS

3 examples of instruments which can be used to develop or sustain interest, prove a point, gather information etc.

| ● MATRIX | ● GRID/WINDOW | ● QUESTIONNAIRE |

FACTORS OR CRITERIA
1
2
3
4
5

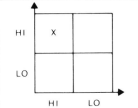

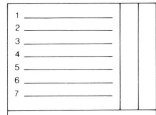

● Decision-making
● Behavioural Analysis
● Plotting of variables
(i.e. who does what to whom)

● To plot a combination of 2 characteristics

● Self-awareness
● Attitude survey
● Polling facts

AUDIO-VISUAL AIDS/EXERCISES

FURTHER READING

- "The Trainer's Pocketbook of ready-to-use exercises", John Townsend, 1993, Management Pocketbooks.

- "Professional Standards for Trainers", Team Training International, 1993. TTI, Isbarrygasse 12, A-1140 Wien, Austria.

- "VHF Communication for Trainers", John Townsend, Journal of European Industrial Training, Volume 13 Number 6, 1989.

- "Team Development Manual", Mike Woodcock, Gower Press 1979

MASTERS FOR REPRODUCTION

INSTRUCTOR FEEDBACK

NAME: _____

Item	Good ✓	Not so good ✗
PREPARATION		
THE 5 W'S		
● WHY? — Analysis of lesson objectives		
● WHAT? — Subject matter level/balance		
● WHO? — Analysis of audience level & expectations		
● WHEN? — Allowance for time of day etc.		
● WHERE? — Allowance for teaching location		
● NOTES (Cards? Paper? Distracting?)		
● STRUCTURE — BANGS? — GUNAR EDEG RAF?		
● ORGANIZATION OF MATERIAL		
PLATFORM SKILLS		
● USE OF VOICE: P A M P E R S (circle not so good)		
● POSTURE		
● EYE CONTACT		
● SPEED		
● MANNERISMS		
● ENTHUSIASM		
● TACT/SENSITIVITY		
● SELF-CONFIDENCE		
● STUDENT PARTICIPATION		
● DISCUSSION LEADING		
● VOCABULARY/LANGUAGE		
● TIMING		
Comments:		
USE OF A/V AIDS		
● FLIP CHART/WHITEBOARD/PINWAND		
● OVERHEAD PROJECTOR		
● SLIDE PROJECTOR		
● TAPE RECORDER		
● VIDEO		
● EXERCISES/INSTRUMENTS		
Comments:		

126

PRESENTATION CHECKLIST

PRESENTATION	①✓	②✓	NOTES
Presentation Cards			
Overheads			
Slides			
Cassettes (Video/Audio)			
Handouts			
Gimmicks			
ACCESSORIES			
Pointer			
Felt Tip Markers			
Overhead Pens			
Masking Tape			
Pen Knife			
Spare Flip Chart			
Plugs/Extensions			
A/V EQUIPMENT			
Flip Chart Stand			
Blackboard/White			
Overhead Projector			
● Spare Lamp ?			
Screen (Tilted)			
Carousel Projector			
● Spare Lamp ?			
● Spare Cartridge ?			
● Remote Control (Ext. ?)			
Cassette Recorder			
Video Equipment			
Amplifier/Speakers			
Microphone			

127

Other Titles in the Pocketbook series

All books priced at £5.95 per copy plus £0.60 postage.   Tapes at £11.75 (inc. VAT & p & p)
Overseas orders : post and packing at cost.

See over for order form

"The Instructor's Pocketbook" is one of a series of Management Pocketbooks. For more details and extra copies, complete the order form (see over) and return to Management Pocketbooks.

About the Author

John Townsend BA, MA, MIPM is Managing Director of Interaction Training Seminars and Workshops. He founded Interaction (which is a member of Team Training International) in 1985 after 20 years of experience in international human resource management positions in the UK, France, the United States and Switzerland. From 1978-1984 he was European Director of Executive Development with GTE in Geneva with training responsibility for over 800 managers in some 15 countries. Mr. Townsend has taught Human Resource Development to graduate students at Webster University in Geneva and acted as a consultant to the ARFORE (Swiss Association of Professional Trainers).

Mr. Townsend has published a number of management and professional guides and regularly contributes articles to leading management and training journals. In addition to teaching a range of specialised management and training skills seminars to multinational clients, he is also a regular speaker at conferences and briefings throughout Europe.

Interaction, Training Seminars and Workshops, Chemin de Bejou, Ornex 01210 Ferney-Voltaire France.

PRINTED IN ENGLAND BY ALRESFORD PRESS, ALRESFORD, HANTS.
EDITIONS: 1st: 1985 2nd: 1987 3rd: 1988 4th: 1990 5th: 1991 6th: 1993

ORDER FORM

Please send me .... copies of "The Instructor's Pocketbook"

.... copies of ....Pocketbook

.... copies of ....Pocketbook

....

Name .... Position ....

Company ....

Address ....

....

....

....

Telephone .... Telex/Fax ....

Management Pocket Books
14 East Street
Alresford
Hampshire SO24 9EE
Tel: (0962) 735573   Fax: (0962) 733637

Please contact the Publisher for bulk
order discounts (10 copies and over)
and further information